LOVE SONGS, SONNETS and SUCHLIKE

by

RICHARD HISLOP

By the same author

A ROSE IN THE BANYAN TREE – a novel – Heinemann 1979

LOVE SONGS, SONNETS and SUCHLIKE

ISBN 0 9536699 0 4

Published by Beaumont College Press
P.O. Box 1225 East Oxford D.O.
OX44 9QE

Printed in Great Britain by William Clowes
NR34 9QE

Distributed by Drum Publishers
P.O. Box 199
Wallingford
OX10 9XR
Tel. and fax 01491 652987

Cover design © Fiona Tedman

CONTENTS

Preface v
Introduction – My Verse vi

I Love songs and sensualities

Love 1
Autumn at Kew 2
Clete Hill I 3
Clete Hill II 4
Clete Hill III 4
Why should I try 5
Fall into my arms 6
Oakley – Whit Sunday 7
I did not mean to love you 8
How should I love you 9
I smile on you 10
If your breasts 11
When the oak be lightning riven 12
The kiss. The memory 13
To Bridget – long after 13
Last poem to Bridget 14
Blue stocking 15
My love is like a red, red rose 16
Departing mistress 17
Love in the roads of the Saints 17
There is a time in life 18
Mill meadows 19
Pemberley Jill 19
After the Dujon 20
Mavis 21
The Secret 21
Villefranche 22
The gilded cage 23

II Bedfordshire

The bells of Bromham 24
To the mayors of Bedford and
    Menton 26
St Paul's Square 27
The girl who waits
    for the Baldock bus 28

Cople Village band 28
The Clapham boys. 29
The girls of Potton 29
Park Avenue –
    song for a summer evening 29
Bromham 30
Sandy 30
Epitaph for a nameless grave in
    Sandy churchyard 31
Sandy churchyard 32
My epitaph 32
Biggleswade 33
Bedford bound 33
The Eastern Counties Bus
    Service 34
Putnoe Woods 35
Queen's Park 36

III London

The city. 37
City canyons 37
The search 38
Mind the doors 39
Miss Arzopardi 40
Commuter 41

IV Oxfordshire

Bladon churchyard 42
Henley 43
Christchurch meadow 44
Dreaming spires 45

V Wider Reflections

Requiem for the future 46
The new world order 49
Four star war 50
Fragment from Kashmir 52

VI Animalia

Zoo-illogical 53
Animal rights – campaigners' song 54
My little sister Marion 57
A sparrow's death 58
Hunting carol 58
Simon the sea serpent 59
Gum Kwot 66
Tortoise and Turtle 66
Terrapin 66

VII Chiefly suchlike

Lullaby for Rachel 67
New Year's Greetings 67

Torreodor Song – new version 68
Salome 69
A Triolet 69
The saying goes 70
Careless woman 70
The widow 70
Beliefs 70
Hymn 70
A promising start 71
Lines of advice 72

Index of first lines 73

Go placidly 74

PREFACE

It is too good an opportunity to miss for providing a preface for one's own poetry, especially when it is a sort of "catalogue résonné" of a lifetime's endeavours. A lifetime's endeavours! Eighty poems? Well . . . yes, inspiration was spasmodic and the gestation period for a poem varied between ten minutes and ten years.

There are other explanations which I should make. For example: I know that it was not Jeremiah but Joshua who marched around Jericho until the walls fell down. But Joshua doesn't oblige the scansion, so biblical verity had to be sacrificed. The "Last Poem to Bridget" is not an epitaph. It expresses my emotions after a vicious car crash in which she could easily have been killed but wasn't: an afterthought on a tragedy which didn't actually happen.

The two men whose works ignited and then sustained my interest in poetry were James Elroy Flecker and A E Housman - I carried books of their complete works with me throughout the war. I still have them, mildewed and battered. It was not unnatural then that my early attempts at verse should be heavily influenced by these two poets.

W H Auden stated that it is quite acceptable for one man to use the conceits of another. I make no apology for doing just that. Later there were other influences, and, indeed, borrowings: Herrick, Hodgson, Masefield and of course Shakespeare. The poem "Zoo-illogical" reveals a debt to a Masefield metre and "Putnoe Woods" is almost painfully Housman. But they were all steps along the way. The earliest verses appear in the Bedfordshire section reflecting my postponed, poetic adolescence in the nineteen fifties and sixties, though the very earliest lines appearing are in the "Fragment from Kashmir", part of a fifty verse saga written there in 1944. The "Go Placidly" stanzas are a versification of a 1692 "Desiderata" discovered in the Old St Paul's Church, Baltimore.

In as far as I have compounded any theory on poetry, it is that it should make oral music. It should conjure up melodies of words which linger in the mind in the same way as an appealing passage of music will do. In the English language we have a fabulous treasure trove of words just waiting to be woven into patterns of distraction and delight.

I hope that my small endeavours will give some distraction and, perhaps, some delight.

RICHARD HISLOP
Oxford, December 1998

INTRODUCTION

MY VERSE

My verse is not profound, enigmatical.
No parable is hidden in its weave.
Elementary scansion that's grammatical
Is all that I endeavour to achieve.
Nor do I claim spurious analytical
Insight to the minds of other men.
An epitaph that tends towards the critical
Is often the best effort of my pen.
But though I say my verse is superficial
You should, at least, be thankful I admit
And do not preach or labour the judicial
And pompous perspicacity of a wit.
So there's my picture - aye, and there's the rub:
A tub thumper without a blooming tub!

I

LOVE SONGS
AND
SENSUALITIES

LOVE

Take it while the sap is rising
Take it while all hope is high
Take it while the petals tremble
Before the flowers fade and die.

Take it while the sun is shining
Take it while the senses flame
Take today and scorn tomorrow
Love has no other name.

AUTUMN AT KEW

Autumn at Kew, in a breath-held stillness
  And the leaves slow turning to yellow and brown,
    Stiff on the trees and mutely falling,
      Softly, softly cascading down.
        Happiness came to our hearts like laughter
          Spreading out on endless wings of song
          As we chased the falling leaves to capture
        And carpet the paths we passed along.
      And the sun was warm and wide that day
      And followed where we led
    And smiled upon our happiness
    And kissed your golden head.
  But all that sun, with infinite caress,
Was not more tender than my tenderness.

CLETE HILL I

To each and all, by love or sorrow torn
The soul from out of suffering is born
As yet the darkest night precedes the dawn,
   Lie still, my love, lie still.

We are but actors on a timeless stage
Mouthing our parts with laughter or with rage
Until the prompter turns the final page,
   He will, my love, he will.

What more is there along this life's arcade
Apart from these sweet moments we have made?
And will they last until desire shall fade?
   Until, my love, until?

The life of day drains slowly from the sky,
Everything that lives will surely die,
The sounds of evening, our love, and you and I,
   They will, my love, they will.

Darkness draws his cloak into the west
And half a fretful world returns to rest -
Perchance to dream? So here upon my breast
   My love, lie still, lie still.

CLETE HILL II

Farewell delightful evening
For dreams must fade and days must end,
And the light be lost to darkness
Like the losing of a childhood friend.

The softly spread of dusk is stretching
Shadows in the harvest-empty fields.
The earth gives up its colours,
Yielding its body as a woman yields.

Stillness yet unfolds from stillness
In the fields beyond the farm
And gentle as the kiss of twilight
Is your sleep-shut head upon my arm.

CLETE HILL III

Stay with me Bridget, here may we
  Recapture that tranquillity
    Which Mary knew when first she came
      Unknown that night to Bethlehem.
      Lie still, I shall not move or speak
        But lay my hand upon your cheek
          And watch the wind of evening weave
            Your soft hair with intricacies
          Soothing with a sure delight
        The silent-foot approach of night.
      Darkness, when your eyes are lit
    With fires which flame in spite of it
  Is softly lulled, and dull with calms
The silence which the night embalms.

WHY SHOULD I TRY?

Why should I try when others fail -
    Others more able with their art
To flourish an accomplished hand
    And limn her features whole or part?

Doubtless they would have me try
    But I could never hope to trace
In stone, or paint or spoken word
    The soft young radiance of her face.

And even though success be mine,
    Then they would only say I lie
And that such grace could only be
    A poet's subtle flattery.

Oh ignorant and pitied man
    Who follows in unmeasured years,
And will not know the loveliness
    And all the glory that is hers.

Sing you this old, archaic song
    And sorrowing, make haste to die,
For you have never seen her smile,
    And never loved her, as have I.

FALL INTO MY ARMS

Fall into my arms beloved,
  Why should you stand up there
    With the silver of the moonlight
      Shining on your hair?
      Why should you stand? For history
      Is full of things that fall:
    The walls of ancient Jericho
At Jeremiah's call.

Night falls, and no-one blames it
  And shadows fall on sand
    And snow will fall at winter
      Whitening the land.
      Silence falls at evening
    And stars fall in the sky,
  Words fall upon unheeding ears
And tears fall from the eye.

Cities, states and empires
  Like apples on the tree
    And yellowed leaves at autumn
      Obey their destiny.
      So why should you resist
      This old world's old alarms?
  Surrender in the evening
And fall into my arms.

She, in his arms, lay
　　Blissfully unaware of time:
　　　Half the day passed overhead.
　　　They did not care.

　　　　Hours were the foam
　　　　　Of falling streams
　　　　　　The bubble bursting dream
　　　　　　　Reborn when lips met lips.

　　　　　　Words were not required.
　　　　　　　There is a speech of touch
　　　　　　　And look. The eyes articulate;
　　　　　　　　And tongue, when met with tongue
　　　　　　　　Speaks in volumes of unwritten thoughts
　　　　　　　Bridging the silence
　　　　　　With the voice of multitudes
　　　　　Yet intimate as one to one.

　　　And so the day slipped past them
　　　　As they lay
　　　Un-noticed and un-noticing.
　　Their's was a century of time
　Within each other's arms
And still they lay
Long after it was dark.

I DID NOT MEAN TO LOVE YOU

I did not mean to love you.
I did not at all set out
To bring this strange and wonderful
State of affairs about.

I did not mean to love you.
My heart was all my own,
My nerve and my emotions
Were mature and fully grown.

It changed with one encounter
A flag of truce shot through,
And now your name pervades my thoughts
And everything I do.

Now, instead of roaming free,
I seek the peace of mind
That leaves our limbs, our love, our lives
Irrevocably entwined.

TO BRIDGET

Of small
  and slender
    stature
      though my
        mistress be,
          let her
            be short
              to others
                but belong
              to me.

TO BRIDGET (expecting Duncan)

Of small
  and slender
    stature
      though she
        no longer be,
          Let her seem
            at large
              to the whole
                wide world
              and still
                belong
                  to me

HOW SHOULD I LOVE YOU?

How should I love you?
Like a virgin wind of spring,
Gentle with the hint of summers yet to come?
With scarcely heard
But vibrant, warm, awakening hum
Of bees now stirring
From a winter's long, dark indolence?
Come, I will kiss
Your sapling limbs
And new with each caress
Give the soft tongue of my tenderness.

How should I love you?
Like a stalwart summer breeze
Broad and mellow throated,
Swollen with the ripened fruit
Of my desiring and rasping
Through the standing corn
And still, by curious custom bound,
As summer's work is done..
Throw its seed upon the ground.

How should I love you?
Like a hapless breeze of autumn
Languorous in the harvest field
Long after the corn has gone?
Lazily I'll soothe
The tremor of your limbs
And close those lovely eyes
With earth-warm kisses.

How should I love you?
Like chill winter's wind
Thrusting deep-shafted
In your autumn innocence?
Come, I will bend your sapling limbs
Beneath my brutal spurring
And wrench a softly plaintive cry
From your long enduring.

I smile on you, for you are lovely,
But *why* should you smile on me?
   You take my love for what it is,
      Roughcut, unkind, uncouth,
       And change it to the gentlest thing
    That ever tempered youth.
I *know* that I should love you
But *why* should you love me?

I smile on you for you are lovely
But *why* should you smile on me?
   I treat the years like errant days
     And hurt you in a thousand ways
     Though not intentionally.
    You? You kiss the minutes when we meet
  And weave them into such strange, sweet
  Patterns of eternity.
I *know* that I should love you
But *why* should you love me?

Perhaps a thousand years from now
Another man will come
And read my words at night, alone
And find his love is like my own
And you - no monument in stone
But standing, - breathing - free.
And he will find, beside your face
A hand stretched out through time and space
To touch and love, like me.
And if he has the soul and heart
To understand the smallest part
Of this great mystery
He'll know, he'll understand
This echo from an ancient land.
And yes! He'll *know why* I did love you
But not *why* you loved me.

IF YOUR BREASTS

If your breasts were towers of ivory
Bold, erect and ivory not flesh,
  My hand would be the architect
    To re-define their classic curve
      And mould their symmetry afresh.

      If your thighs were golden sands
        Stretching long-limbed by the sea,
          My undisputed hand would trace
            Along their sandy sinewy grace;
              Nor all the sea's vast ebb and flow
              Would quite erase their print although
            The sands of ages sift and blow
        In ceaseless elegy.

      If our love were a meteor
     Alive in the wide night sky,
    Its incandescent fire would flame
   Into the ages without name -
  Would bridge the centuries of tears
And all a million, million years
Would never see it die.

When the oak be lightning riven
    And the thundery torrents roar,
And the waves, wild-winded driven,
    Hurl their ranks upon the shore;

When the deserts drain the oceans
    And the ice the forests numb
And terrestrial commotion
    Strike the starving people dumb;

When the world in aberration
    Seeks the ending that it must
And every single nation
    Turns to perish in the dust;

Then I say - then only,
    In a murmur half divine,
Earthly echoes, long and lonely
    Will repeat your name and mine;

And when all has been dismembered
    And swept like chaff before the wind
Our love will be remembered
    In some superhuman mind.

THE KISS

You turned and kissed me where I stood
Just the way I hoped you would
With rougish charm, devoid of guile,
Wide mouthed and with gentle smile.
Your lips spoke more than lips should speak
And lingered softly on my cheek.

THE MEMORY

Not with a sigh you gave yourself to me
But with some youthful fancy broken free
Loosed on wings untried, unknown before
Trembling at each beat that urges more
With laughter and with happiness untold
And framed with swirling hair like burnished gold.

TO BRIDGET ....LONG AFTER

As roses weep that have no eye to favour
So you must weep for me when I am gone,
For who will paint and your perfection savour
In ceaseless words of praise when you are left alone?
The mirror may be true in its reflection
But can only take the image of the day,
And cannot bring to life in recollection
Those golden glorious limbs of yesterday.
Only in my mind can it be measured,
That unsurpassed fecundity of youth,
And only in my mind can it be treasured
And linger on like some eternal truth.
So weep not for passing beauty but weep for me
Whose fragile words must frame its elegy.

LAST POEM TO BRIDGET

There is a cruel emptiness
now that you are gone,
like a shadow-darkened garden
in which the sun once shone.

And the essence of your being
beside me all those years
dissolves with mists of evening
as in a vale of tears.

No more of loving laughter
and the soft arms of delight,
and lonely now, I wander
towards the coming night.

And yet perhaps, in worlds beyond
where lost souls take release,
if your spirit hand may touch my hand
we'll find eternal peace.

'J.S.' - BLUE STOCKING

Have you lost love, O intellectual one
Demurely wrapt in scholarly discourse?
And have you no time for affection,
The subtle blend of passion and remorse?

Oh true you weave impressive argument
And put my sorry babbling to disgrace,
But have you never felt soft lips intent
Or lost an evening in a long embrace?

I too have searched for knowledge - not in books -
And gazed all day into another's eyes,
And slowly turned the pages of her looks
And come away - oh wonderfully wise.

Can we not learn to love and part as friends
And smile on life before its chapter ends.

MY LOVE IS LIKE A RED, RED ROSE
(A SONG)

My love is like a red, red rose
    That sings a summer melody
        And brings on every breeze that blows
            a song to me.

Her voice is like a turtle dove
    That soothes the day when sun goes down
        And moves in moments that I love,
            every frown.

She stays like meadow sweetness in a stream
And plays like dancing shadows in a dream
But when shadows and the dream have gone
        my love stays on.

Her touch is light as thistledown
    That drifts across the evening land
        And rests as lightly as a kiss
            upon my hand.

Her lips are like a sweet red wine
    That bring to mind some sunny skies
        And when they come to rest on mine
            .... time flies.

I'll ask no more of any passer-by
And bask under her eternal sky
For when summer and the sun have gone
        my love stays on.

And so I end my simple song
    And really do not care who knows
        For though the world may say I'm wrong
            My love is like a red, red rose.

LOVE IN THE ROADS OF THE SAINTS

The Gods she followed were death-foreboding
and darkly obsessed with a sense of sin,
mine were of life and love and laughter
with wide arms ever welcoming.

Hers were of shame and retribution -
no wonder it was that she turned my way,
for mine were of joy and love returning
and lingering, like a summer's day.

High at the altar of her surrender
the ancient superstition died,
and there on the bed of her undoing
she stretched her sleeping limbs and sighed.

DEPARTING MISTRESS

She said it would be best for her to go
And looked me in the eyes with cold disdain.
I said it might, for who was I to know?
Who never knew restraint could not restrain.
Her lips were trembling as she spoke, I saw
Her handkerchief was clenched behind her back.
I shrugged a brief reply and said no more
But went upstairs with her to help her pack.
We taxied to the station, found the train
Was overdue, that she would have to wait
In a waiting room, its windows blind with rain
And fire of dull indifference in the grate.
And there we kissed goodbye. It was a kiss
Of warm and moist antithesis.

There is a time and place in life
For women such as you,
Who place no bonds about a man
But love him as they will and can
And make him feel a king.
Love him, as they will and can
With neither avarice nor plan
And hold his love by bonds
Sometimes no finer than
The merest thread of love
And some instinctive understanding.

You may never know the happiness
Of children at your knees.
That unexplained primeval joy
Of women for a girl or boy
And sharing through the passing years
With constant jostling joys and fears
The laughter bathed with hope and tears
And intermittent pain.
You may know none of these.

But with your love you can create
Kingdoms that were not there before.
To make a man reach out and climb
To endless ecstasy sublime
And come to terms with tide and time
That know no written law.
To make him turn again and shake
The corners of his world and break
His wild and widest waves of love
On some far distant shore.

You know I cannot give to you
The things which really are your due
But then you asked for none of these.
Forgive me then, for loving you
And treating you the way I do.
Forgive this battle-scarred and weary man
And love me as those great women can
Who have no children at their knees.

MILL MEADOWS

Kiss me
while
the going's good
at midnight
by the river.
I am a man of flesh
and blood
and will not last forever.

Turn your back
on wrong and right
that rend
the world asunder,
your limbs
were meant for me tonight,
and will not perish under.

So love me
whilst none other may,
stretch out
this hour
and then forget,
tomorrow
is another day
and bears no malice of regret.

PEMBERLEY JILL

Jill jilted me! I'm sad to say
Our love affair is ended.
We were so friendly yesterday
But now I've been suspended.

Of course, I knew it couldn't last
But 'twould have been less ill
When finally we had to part,
If I had jilted Jill.

If only my love
    had been fine and fair
        and not imbued
            with shame, perhaps
        I could forget her
    or at least
remember her name.
But my love was a lust
    that overwhelmed
        her inadequate defence
            as she lay
        like a lovely flower unfolding
unguarded innocence.
So shapely, firm
    and lithely limbed
        and so willing for caress
            she reached her sudden climax
        with submissive eagerness.
We played and stretched
    those vagrant hours
        through the darkness of the night
            and parted only
        when the dawn's
    cool ardour came to light.
And now she lies
    with memories
        half fantasy, half truth
            of wide-eyed
        wistfully wonderful
    and distant days of youth.

MAVIS

Mavis, gentle Mavis
How do I view you now
With the wrinkles of so many years
Escutcheoned on your brow?
Do you recall that distant day
When you and I were wed?
Not in church or chapel
Or in the marriage bed
But in the lush green fields of spring
Beside the River Ouse
When maidenheads were gladly lost
But never ask me whose.

December 1997

THE SECRET

We have a secret no one shares
A startling moment set aside
That stalked and caught us unawares
And left such happiness to hide

Not for us the open smile
The frank and innocent caress
But guarded words and all the while
Companionship in loneliness.

VILLEFRANCHE

I sat
    where we sat
    those years ago
    when life was slow and wide and clear
    and the things we loved and held most dear
    were one,
    and the sun
    shone down
    and warmed my face
    but the warmth I knew in a different place
    was gone.

I heard
    the sea's
    soft ebb and flow
    stretch up the beach, although
    the sound that I yearned to hear
    was far
    and just as far as the sea was near,
    and your voice
    unlike the sea
    in a distant land-locked memory.

I stretched
    my hand
    to touch your hand
    where your hand was meant to be,
    and the nothingness that met me there
    had not the half of my despair,
    and the sight and the sound and the touch of you
    and the happiness I thought I knew
    were lost
    as perhaps
    they were meant to be
    in a remorseless sea.

THE GILDED CAGE
(A SONG)

Can you hear the singing bird
Singing in the tree
And does she sing that fetching song
Because she flies so free
Or yearns for love like me.

Take a piece of paper
And crayons, gold and grey
And draw a cage, a gilded cage
In which your love can stay
And sing throughout the day.

Then take your cage into the wood
Into the open air
And hang it high upon a tree
For all the world to stare
And see it swinging there.

But if you sense some discord
And sadness in her songs
Open wide the cage's door
And set her free forever more
To fly where she belongs.

Then if your love flies back to you
Tear that cage apart
You never will have need of it
Destroy it, every part.
You hold her in your heart.

II

BEDFORDSHIRE

THE BELLS OF BROMHAM

I've come ten thousand miles to hear those bells
Break the peace of evening with a brazen smile
And sweep in meadow measured peals
Along the river, up and down a mile.
Soft airs of summer spread them wide and near -
North to the village, southward to the road,
Drown for a moment in the Roman weir
Or mute them strangely in the scented wood.
They make their stand against the brutal years
That crucify mankind in every age:
They peal with hope, or toll like sullen tears
For shattered dreams and smother futile rage.
They also view with grave, impartial eye
Those brave, sad years when men march out to die.

For I marched out, and thought I'd never hear
The bells of any English church again.
I learned to stand my ground and live with fear
But did not know our victory was in vain.
We thought to save that which we could not save
To defend things indefensible
And left behind so many an unmarked grave
To prove all human dreams incomprehensible.
Once there was a time I swore I heard
Those bells ring sweetly through the shell-raked trees
But when the firing faded nothing stirred
In jungle still as dead men's memories.
Oh envied bells of Bromham by the river
My song will die and yours go on for ever.

My song will die but your wide peals will live
To generations in unmeasured time
Preserving in the melody they give
A living speech which will outlast my rhyme:
For human voices leave no echoes here
No lingering tones which will repulse decay
The lips which whisper this into your ear
Will soon be past, and vague as yesterday.
The years stretch onward like an endless plain
And yet no famine, fear or fever quite dispels
The bold and desperate march of man
Whilst somewhere in the distance beat those bells
To ease the aching heart, and dull the sting
Of wars and strife and human suffering.

Bromham, 1947

[25]

TO THE MAYORS OF BEDFORD AND MENTON

If I should die in Bedford
find me a fenland grave,
and let the good earth nurture
the limbs it could not save.

Let rain and storm and tempest
by the bleak north-easters driven
diffuse into that precious soil
the gift by England given.

But should I die in Menton,
with or without renown,
then take me to the cemetery
that lies above the town.

Find me a place between those stones
for this, my last endeavour
and let the warm, wide southern sun
smile on my grave forever.

1989

Back
from church
the people
come,
the sane,
the stupid,
the hum-very-drum
and as they
walk
I hear
their bones
clicking
on
the cobble-stones
and cobbles
make
such fearful
holes
in
their
thinly
welted
souls.

TO THE GIRL WHO WAITS FOR THE BALDOCK BUS

I like the way you stand, you silken slut,
It would do credit to a woman twice your age.
I like the stylish way you pace and strut
 As though the grimy street were just a stage.
I like the way you hold your head erect,
 The careless way in which you peer and pause
 And use your lithe-limbed body to effect
As if unconscious of the glance it draws.
I like the way you fling your fabulous hair
 Back from the shoulder with a subtle twist
And smiling, bring your silken blouse to bear
Taut and thin across your petulant breast.
 Perhaps it's better, if you want the truth,
 To lose one's innocence before one's youth.

Biggleswade 1948

COPLE VILLAGE BAND

harsh
like a ranting bark vibrating
the brass
flared out
between the houses
of the square
and the thumping thud
of the drum
pulsating
out of the village
into the country air

THE CLAPHAM BOYS

The Clapham boys are spunky
And will fight with anyone
But will always pick you up
And dust you down when they have done.

The Clapham girls, on the other hand,
Are wine of a different cup
And are much more readily inclined
To lie you down and dust you up.

THE GIRLS OF POTTON

The girls of Potton, Sandy, Beds.,
Have such delightful golden heads
And lissom limbs and lovely eyes-
Like dew pools deep in paradise.
But stone the crows! The noise they make
Gives the chap the belly ache.
I'm sure the Gods have now repented
Such grace, atrociously accented.
Aye, a fool or deaf, is he who weds
A girl from Potton, Sandy, Beds.

PARK AVENUE -
SONG FOR A SUMMER
EVENING

Softly the branches ply
  Whispering eternally
    Under my window.
Faintly, I know not where,
Far from its woodland haunt
I hear the cuckoo chant.
Lingering, now it fades
Silence again invades,
Night turns, wide and deep
And I to my restless sleep
While branches softly ply
  Whispering eternally
    Under my window.

BROMHAM

I cannot hear the cuckoo calling
Half-fields off beyond the woodland
Feel the green-warm scent of summer
Steal across the silent pasture
See the meadow breeze far from me
Sweeping through the wheat and barley
Hear your voice adistant singing
Like a bird amid the rushes
Feel your hand upon my shoulder
Speaking with a steady pressure
See your eyes deny the rumour
That our love will be forgotten.

SANDY

The chimney stacks of Sandy
Are such that you might see
Along the vale of Paradise
By the shores of Galilee:

They stand, alone and clustered,
Cerise and brown and grey,
The sentinels of evening,
The heralds of the day.

From far, from town and country,
The people come to stand
And watch the shades of evening
Unfolding on the land

And see the stacks of Sandy
Catch the declining day
And brickwork haze and glimmer
And fall to dark away.

EPITAPH
FOR A NAMELESS GRAVE IN SANDY CHURCHYARD

Lie here
un-named, unknown
in shallow rest
no cross
of bronze
or stone
upon
your breast.

Lie here
un-known, un-named
no thought amiss
whatever
man has
claimed
he comes
to this.

Whatever
he has claimed
of glories won,
no worse
to die
un-named
and lie
alone.

No worse
to die at last when
life has flown,
to slip
the bitter
past
un-named,
un-known.

SANDY CHURCHYARD

This counterpane of sorrows
Is close upon your chest
For you no more tomorrows
Will stir you from your rest.

For you no threat of judgment
Need mar the sleep you take,
No further sixth commandment
For you to keep or break.

Man's judgment has been meted
On your unhallowed brow,
No afterthought compassion
From me could mend that now.

So let the dew, adorning
This grass-bound quilt of thine,
Rebuke the endless morning
As tears which might be mine.

MY EPITAPH

What use of pride when I am dead?
Give me humility instead
Let its calm, soft footfall sound
Upon my grave, here in the ground.

BIGGLESWADE

I saw a woman with a lovely face in
Biggleswade - very much to my surprise, for
Biggleswade is not the sort of place to find beauty in
any shape or guise. In that drab and dismal town
there were so few attractive things, but she - she had
a lovely face, a tilt of head, a way of walk that gave
her a charming, sweet and unaffected grace. It
seemed she had some inner radiance, some secret of
her own that no-one knew and brought to bleak
Biggleswade, by chance, a loveliness to be seen by
all too few. As I wondered what it was I had not
learned about the ways of women and of men, a child
ran, clutching, to her side. She smiled and took its
hand. I knew her secret then.

BEDFORD BOUND

A small brow-beaten man
He was, waiting for the bus.
I wondered if he was Bedford bound,
Or just from bad to wus.
He stood beside the Bedford Road
So pathetically plain
And hunched in desperation
Against the rain
That if I could, I would have pitied him.
That's all I can recall.
But I wondered what he did in life
And why he lived at all.

Six days a week, the whole year through
The motor bus has plied
To bring to Bedford town anew
Folk from the countryside.

The whole year through, a week's six days,
Each motor bus sets down
In villages and country ways
The people of the town.

Summer, autumn, winter, spring,
From *here*, from left to right,
They fetch themselves from *there* to bring
Them back again each night.

They travel happily enough
And never reason why
They're made of such ephemeral stuff
To shuttle till they die.

For soon or late, if truth be known
The long black bus will come
And take them out of Bedford town
And never bring them home.

PUTNOE WOODS

To Putnoe Woods in springtime
   The lover and his lass
Come out from Clete and Bedford
   The sunny rides to pass
   Or linger in the grass.

And walking there at evening
   I see them pair on pair
And if they look towards me
   Return each curious stare
   With eyes that cry 'beware'.

Alas, they do not heed me,
   With sighs their dreams devour
And lift from mouths unthirsted
   In passions of the hour
   Their lips, which are not sour.

I, and I 'tis only
   Who sees what summer brings
Who knows what grief unbounded
   Will mute the thrush that sings
   With tears and sufferings.

A zoom bazoo bazoo
flew
around the empty rubbish mound,
it drew
tiny rivulets of sound
around, around,
and moved the leaves
like sleepless children.

The zoom bazoo bazoo
grew
into a breathless, morning noise
it drew soft ragged tears from toys
and empty tins.

Sweet, fresh wind upon the skin
socks slow slipping down the shin
rain as strong as back street gin
it fits, it fits
no softer song was ever sung
and no gold banners ever hung
on garbage tips.

Zoom bazoo bazoo
the children knew
and you did too
those years ago
in the back streets of the town.

The grey cloud of those endless days
so many years
so many towns ago.

Look down
beyond your soaking socks
and see the clouds
like silvered ships
in pools between the yellow mud.

III

LONDON

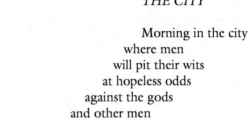

THE CITY

Morning in the city
where men
will pit their wits
at hopeless odds
against the gods
and other men
who pit them
and
where only half
the men
with bowler hats
have heads
to fit them.

THE CITY CANYONS

Higher and higher
in the city
they build with steel and stone
to show that
man's salvation
is not by faith alone;
and deep in those city canyons
where the sun
so seldom breaks
men add
subtract and multiply
and sell
their souls for steaks.

I asked the way
to Heaven
from a London
railway porter;
he said he thought
that I would find
the Inner Circle
shorter.

I asked the way
to Heaven
from a woman
in the dark;
she smiled
and coyly mentioned
an address
in Holland Park.

I asked the way
to Heaven
from a man
I thought a priest;
he said that I
would have to die
like any other
beast.

So I asked
a large policeman
who, without
the slightest fuss,
smiled and very gently
pushed me
underneath
a bus.

MIND THE DOORS

"Mind the doors," he said distinctly,
"Mind the doors" I heard him say,
  And my heart went out to greet him
For the frank, determined way
  In which he said, quite plainly,
  All that he had got to say.

  Not "Minnarup" or "Minawar",
It was not snarled or slurred,
  With precise enunciation
He pronounced each single word.
  "Mind the doors," was what he shouted,
  "Mind the doors," was what we heard.

  In these days, when politics
Are thrust down people's throats
  And lies dressed up like cottage pies
To win deciding votes
  The 'noes' may stream with many a beam
  But 'ayes' still have their motes,

  Be thankful, be much comforted
That there is one man in the crowd
  Who gets his message over
In accents clear and loud,
  And of plain-speaking Englishmen
  All England should be proud.

  So wherever in the annals
Of our history are found
  Praise for English bravery,
Let the loudest praises sound
  For an unknown railway porter
  On the London underground.

1951

Miss Arzopardi, though your face
Is of some dark, non-British race,
Let me explain:
Odds on, we shall not meet again.
Tomorrow this five-thirty tide
May not sweep you to my side
And press you very close to me
Which somehow makes me feel you're mine
For two stops, on the Central Line.

Miss Arzopardi,
Some distant sun has smiled on you
To make that honey-coloured hue
In skies of bluer blue by far
Than ever fog-bound London's are.
Take me, take me by the hand
Out of this over-crowded land.
Let me find your lips' caress
In warm and naked happiness,
Where the sun is ever by the sea
And time itself is meaningless
And love goes on and on and on
Long after life itself has gone.

Miss Arzopardi,
It's nice to know you cared
In this brief moment we have shared;
Farewell, sweet thing, goodnight to you,
I'm changing here, for Waterloo.

COMMUTER

There is no majesty for man who stands
Straining at the strap. His life is drab
With discontent, surrendered to the hands
At controls in the isolated cab.
Tensed, and swaying at the slightest lurch,
A sort of praying mantis in decline,
For this is his evening service, this the church
Of his devotions - the Piccadilly line.
He turns his head but he can only hear
Mutilated voices buffeted around,
Human vagaries of tongue and ear
Being slowly and mechanically drowned.
Ignoble man, divinely uninspired
Harassed, hungry, overworked and tired.

IV

OXFORDSHIRE

BLADON CHURCHYARD

So great a man lies buried here, there is
No need to raise a monument of stone.
Words and deeds, those monuments are his:
They stand gigantic and they stand alone.
Never, in all the course of history,
Has one man stood so stalwart to defend
The threatened flame of human liberty
And none has seen such victory in the end.
From his countryman he drew their finest hour
And offered only blood and toil and tears
Yet nourished hope and faith and staying power
Throughout the long, dark tempest of those years.
He gave the lion's roar - made others hear the call
And with his greatness made heroes of us all.

1996

Young woman in the yellow dress
You are much bolder, I confess,
Than young things were when I was young.
Not that the girls I moved among
Were in the least bit prude or staid,
But it was a different game we played.
"Decorum" was the basic rule.
And I conformed like any fool.
Conformed at least, as best I could.
I was not wholly bad. Nor good.
But you, young thing, with care-free ways
Make mockery of those distant days,
So blithely, sweetly unaware
With fabulous golden mane of hair
And laughing face and lovely eyes
Like dewpools under summer skies.
Yes, you with your beguiling ways
Ignorant of an old man's gaze
Seem wildly indiscreet and yet-
Such an innocent coquette.
Is it your young exuberance
Which draws my more than casual glance
Rekindling half-forgotten fires
Of faint and fanciful desires.
Enchanting sylph, drink up your Pimms.
Stretch out those adolescent limbs
And flaunt them for my eyes' caress
In all your pride and loveliness.

1996

CHRISTCHURCH MEADOW

Who will walk in the meadow
a thousand years from now
if it be not stiff with houses
or rough beneath the plough?

But who will they be? The people?
holy men or kings?
or insubstantial shadows
of my imaginings?

Will they be men with hearts of
    stone
with little time for others,
or patient, honest country folk
and caring wives and mothers?

Or lovers locked in long embrace
responsive to each touch,
ignorant of passing time,
nor caring very much?

Will they have known ambition's
    spur
and reached the goals they set
or struggle on defiantly
bold believers yet?

But have they some remembrance
of our sweet English tongue
and a little understanding
of the ghosts they walk among,

Then we shall all rest easy
and smiling, kiss their hands,
with kisses light as thistledown
in sunlit summer lands.

For we once walked the meadow
and learned, in fits and starts
companionship and loving
and yearning in our hearts.

And pride we had, in country,
and strength to share its pain
throughout its long and glorious
    years
which will not come again.

They may not hear our voices
nor see us as they pass
nor ever come to notice
our footprints in the grass.

But if they pause whilst walking
to quaff this English air
with pride in their inheritance
then we shall not despair.
Our hearts and souls are there.

Oxford 1998

[44]

DREAMING SPIRES

The teeming streets of Oxford
Are paved with dreams and gold
And hopes and fears which passing years
May banish, so I'm told.

And youths do come aplenty
From places far afield
To find what fundamental truths
Those dreaming spires may yield.

Some will take its wisdom
And wear it like a crown
Finding laws to suit their cause
Which never let them down.

Others, and there are many,
Wilfully or by chance,
Will wrap around their shoulders
Abysmal ignorance.

Yet all may rise in stature
Of riches or renown
And look back fondly on those days
They spent in Oxford town.

In cities of antiquity
Whose names are half forgot,
Saints and sages of those days
In their multifarious ways,
Struggled, as like as not,

To pass on their perception
Of how this world should be
Revealing to the chosen few
Paths to eternity.

Taxila, Alexandria,
Heidelburg and Rome
Flourished their convictions
Like beacons in a storm.

Yet never managed to resolve
The universal plan
Of whether man creates his Gods
Or God created man.

So look you back on Oxford
Of dreaming spires and river
Where enlightenment is there to find
And youthful doubts are left behind
And faith and hope become entwined
And dreams drift on for ever.

Oxford 1998

V

WIDER REFLECTIONS

REQUIEM FOR THE FUTURE

When all is said and all is done
And battles fought and lost or won
And the victor and the vanquished stand
Aghast upon the ravaged land
Who is there left to take the strain
To stoop and build things up again?
Both the coward and the brave
Must struggle out and seek to save
Whatever things they can
From the vast savag'ries of man
They must toil and sweat and strive,
Merely because they are alive.
They must plough and plant and sow
And reap whatever crops may grow
And from the spores of death must draw
Some semblance of their life before.
But there is yet another seed,
Mankind's most single, precious need:
They must woo and they must wed
They must take a wife to bed
And from the loins of love or lust
Regenerate their nation's trust
Hoping in future years to find
Quietness for the unquiet mind
And come, perhaps, to understand
The softness of a young child's hand,
Lovingly kiss away their tears
And learn to calm their childish fears
And find that simple things can please
And love can blossom by degrees.

But let them know, the risk is there.
And tell them so. Make them aware!
For deep, deep, deep in the heart of man
There lies an urge which, if it can,
Will rise again and sweep away
The patient gains of yesterday
Re-enacting every scene
Every terror that has been
Unleashed on earth since time began.
Such is the waywardness of man.
They will not know their die is cast
Moulded by passions of the past.
For all the children that they breed
Will slowly learn their father's creed
And in whatever tongue they claim
God will have a different name
With different truths and different prayers
And different ways to set affairs
And different offerings to give
To regulate the way they live.
Hapless and unaware they'll come
With the slow tapping of the drum
To follow, blindly, one and all,
Religious or political
Priest or president or King,
Tragically unquestioning.

Yes, hapless, unaware they'll come
To the slow tapping of the drum.
A single cause, or complex mix
Of God, race, land or politics
Is all it really ever needs
To germinate those dormant seeds
Of discord, animosity and hate
Eternal in the human state.
Then, faintly but ominously plain,
They'll hear that fearful sound again
Fitfully, then more and more -
The howling of the dogs of war.

What can they do but dumbly stand
And try to defend their native land?
Defend such faith as they possess
With deep and growing bitterness
Blindly placing all their hope
On king or president or pope
In whose words or battle-cry
Their sole salvation seems to lie?
And while the wheel of fortune turns
A Hamburg or a London burns
Another Somme or Paschendale
Is fought, but on a larger scale.
Then there is nothing left to say.
Fanatics will have won the day.
Ten thousand times ten thousand dead
Are mute when victory prayers are said.
So what can they do but hide their fears
Ignore the pattern of past years
And as their mothers did before,
Cheer their children off to war.

October 1990

THE NEW WORLD ORDER

So this is the new world order:
The missiles and the bombs
And later, when its over,
The building of the tombs
And tearful hand-on-heart remorse
And pious protestation
That there ever was recourse
To such brutal devastation?

The jackal thieves or kills for food
Consumes it, bones and all
But humans show a different mood
When they hear their conscience call.
The taunted rattlesnake will strike
Not in anger but in fear
Humans murder when they like
And never shed a tear.

In the congress of the nations
When pros and cons are weighed
Do they take consideration
How the games of war are played?
Do they kneel and ask forgiveness
From the gods of their creation
Before they blast their fellow men
To stark extermination.

1990

Rejoice! There'll be an end to dying.
The drums of death will cease to roll
And Saudi sheikhs be safe in buying
An English village whole.

Will they put flowers on John Scott's grave
    When the desert war is done
And the petrol prices he fought to save
    Be saved - depending who's won?

Will the Belgian burgher show remorse
    And will he think it's fair,
As he settles down to his second course,
    That John Scott is lying there?

Will the Texan farmer shed a tear
    As he starts his second car
And drives ten miles for a crate of beer?
    (Ten miles is not very far).

Will a distant sheikh in Araby
    Shake desert sand from his gold
And thank his god there'll always be
    Soldiers who do what they're told?

John Scott was not the bravest of men
    Not right for the army at all
No medal winner for sure, but then
    He did his duty, that's all.

No Christian burial for John,
    Because, at the place where he fell
In the sacred land he died upon
    He was classed as an infidel.

Flowers won't grow in desert sand
    As Scott's wife and mother know
Nor ever will they understand
    The reason he had to go.

The price of oil may rise or slump
   And no more lives be lost
But will the forecourt petrol pump
   Display the human cost?

Rejoice! There'll be an end to dying
The drums of death will cease to roll
And Saudi sheikhs be safe in buying
An English village whole.

In late August, a newspaper reported that another 8,000 British troops had been detailed for service in the Gulf War. On a different page of the same paper it was reported that a Saudi sheikh had bought a complete English village for £8 million.

September 1990

FRAGMENT FROM KASHMIR

Where Indian princes walked and passed their day
And laughed and slept and kept their honeyed wives,
There I pitched my tent and humbly lay
Beside the walls which once had shared their lives

The ancient splendour of that fallen stone
Was not a mite less noble where it lay;
The cracked and ruined fountains all had known
A majesty of some much earlier day

And lying there, immutably alone
Whilst sunset, westing, struck its dying beams
I fashioned it again, rebuilt it stone on stone
And peopled it with fancies of my dreams.

                                        Kashmir 1944

VI

ANIMALIA

ZOO-ILLOGICAL

Duck-billed platypus dancing on a dandelion
and smoking a Havana on a Sunday afternoon
chuckled confidentially
and then began mechanically
unravelling spaghetti with a wobbly wooden spoon.

Grumpy hippopotamus, with mud-caked proboscis,
munching to the music of the Sugar Plum F,
sat on his parabola
(which buckled most alarmingly)
and murmured next to nothing in a squeaky treble clef.

Lonely little toucan, appearing from a poster,
blushing at the lyrics of an intimate review,
raised a point of order,
a beer mug and a bowler,
and wondered what it really was that only two can do.

Multi-coloured mugwump (the lesser bird of paradise)
doodling absent-mindedly with pale green ink,
sang a little aria
with obvious embarrassment,
and wondered what the devil made the sea-skunk stink.

ANIMAL RIGHTS – campaigners' song

Animals, animals we must unite
Stand together and take up the fight,
Considerate treatment is all that we ask
It's really not such a difficult task.

Elephants must come along
To put the world to rights.
Yes, the elephants must come along
Trumpeting their old school song
And stamping with their feet.
And all the gnats must loudly hum
Making pandemonium
Sound very, very sweet.

Crocodiles, without a tear
Must raise a subterranean cheer
And lash their tails in fun,
And porcupines, with flashing quills,
Like happy harpists, harping trills,
Must twang them, every one.

Deep in the jungle's highest growths
The laziest of one-toed sloths
Must even twitch a tail.
The rarest and the meekest bird
Must make quite sure his song is heard
(Even pheasants need not quail)
The crane must lift his higher notes
And pelicans gargle in their throats
Like water in a pail.

The lizard, newt and toad and frog
From stream and pond and boggy bog
Must splash and bay like bulls,
And eagles, in their eyries high
Must all emit an eerie cry
And swans must sing like gulls.

Even gum-kwots – usually dumb,
Must manage just a little hum
And sway upon the trees.
Even, yes, the common spud,
Tone deaf and up to eyes in mud,
Must chip in graciously.
And sperm whales must arise and spout
To show they know what it's about
And carbonise the sea.

Centipedes, ten thousand strong
Must fall in step and march along
Singing Kipling's "Boots"
The owl must give all feathered friends
A final chance to make amends
And humming birds give hoots.

And hammer headed sharks must fill
The seas with hammering until
They make the anvil chorus.
And grizzly bears must grizzle louder
Making black and brown bears prouder
And even quite sonorous.

In darkest caves the agile bat
Must spread his wings - a trifle flat
And squeak a little higher
The lyre bird must strum a tune
From dawn until the afternoon
To prove he's not a liar.

In Antarctica's wide expanse
King Penguins must begin to dance
And sea-lions too must take their chance
Making waves of semi-quavers.
All India should resound to hoots
Of operatic bandicoots
In minims of all flavours.

In dulcet tones, or tongue in cheek
From every snout or gill or beak
From largest roar to smallest squeak
The whole cacophony of sound
Must fill the air and shake the ground
Emboldening the meek.

Then elephants can come along
To put the world to rights.
Yes, elephants can come along
Trumpeting their old school song
And stamping with their feet.
And all the gnats can loudly hum
Making pandemonium
Sound very, very sweet.

Animals, animals we must unite
Stand together and take up the fight,
Considerate treatment is all that we ask
It's really not such a difficult task

MY LITTLE SISTER, MARION

My little sister, Marion
  Was really rather vile.
When she was very, very young
  She caught a crocodile

She took it out to parties
  But she wouldn't let it sing
And only smacked it harder
  When it cried like anything.

In spite of all her loving care
  It developed frightful habits.
It wouldn't eat its rabbit pie
  (My sister kept rabbits)

She put it in the bathroom
  To see if that would curb it
And father wouldn't shave for weeks
  Rather than disturb it.

Once our village neighbourhood
  Was full of little boys
Who often stole our strawberries
  And made a lot of noise

But since we've had the crocodile
  The gardener's all smiles
You cannot find a little boy
  For miles and miles and miles.

Then when my sister came of age,
  She stunned it with a sandbag.
Whatever else my sister needs,
  She never needs a handbag.

A SPARROW'S DEATH

Pathetic little sparrow must you die
Upon the path so disconcertingly?
With beak agape, and gasping now for breath
Is this the way to welcome timely death?
Yet man must come to this undisguised
Distraught flotsam on life's last breathing tide
However high we flew, however wide
We stretched our wings, however hard we tried
And failed or half succeeded, whatever dearth
That in our time we suffered, we also fall to earth
And so accept our final worth.

HUNTING CAROL
(to the tune of Good King Wenceslas)

Bring my gun and cartridges
Bring my gun dogs hither,
I'm off to shoot some partridges
Down beside the river.
In this season of good cheer
I'll be out there trying
To satisfy my urge to kill
Anything that's fli-i-ing.

SIMON, THE SEA-SERPENT

Have you ever heard the tale
Of how a serpent, like a whale
But not exactly, swam
Up the Thames to Caversham
And then to Oxford, where
With incalculable care
And the sweetest of all graces
He watched the races?

Ever since a tiny tot
A little, spongy, inky blot
Puffing out and puffing in
Swimming by his mother's fin
He'd heard the tale of Oxford - how
Boats with apples in the prow
Raced against each other
(As he raced against his mother).

So when he reached a goodly age
He made the journey stage by stage
To London, where the river came
(Illustrious with illustrious name)
Tidal and tumultuous
Past those towns which seem to us to be
Models of mediocrity.
Not so to him. But I will tell
The story as it all befell.

This inquisitive Sea Serpent
Was of ancient Scottish stock
And discovered just how hard it was
To travel through a lock.

Not though his seamanship was bad
For in her early teens
He'd served a long apprenticeship
Alongside Cunard Queens.

And had a mate's certificate
Which stated all the facts
Signed with purple signatures
And sealed with sealing wax.

But the Lock-keeper at Richmond
Just wouldn't let him through.
He said "I must receive an order
For everything I do.

I've studied regulations
'Cos I learned to read at school
And they don't apply to serpents.
I'd hate to break the rule.

You see, you're not a steamer,
You're not a paddle-boat,
You haven't got a Plimsoll Line
Showing when you float.

You're not a heavy-laden barge,
You're not a little tug,
You're nothing that goes 'splash' or 'splosh'
And nothing that goes 'chug'."

Simon was so sorry
And sobbed some bitter tears
Which created much confusion
By flooding all the weirs.

"I want to go to Oxford,
I want to see the Bumps,
I've had inoculations
And I haven't had the mumps.

Couldn't you oblige me,
Just ignore what orders say?
I will work the gates myself
If you will look the other way."

But the Lock Keeper was stubborn:
"I just can't let you through
But I'll phone the port of London
And ask them what to do."

So he telephoned to London
Explaining to his chief,
But after waiting ages
The reply was very brief.

"No," he said, "Headquarters
Have looked it up in law
And say this sort of problem
Has not occurred before:

And though they'd like to sympathise
They insist that I obey
All that standing regulations
             ...Have to say.

You see, it simply can't be done,
We wouldn't know the charge,
Not even if you happened
To be carried in a barge."

"Carried in a barge!" he cried,
"Why, of course! That's it!
You could travel up to Oxford,
But it'll cost you quite a bit."

Simon thereupon produced
From underneath a fin,
A purse of Scottish seaweed
Fastened with a pin.

"In the summer holidays
When I'm feeling bold,
I dive for treasure galleons
And often bring up gold."

The trip was thereupon arranged
And bargees and a barge
Towed him up to Oxford
For quite a modest charge.

The colleges all welcomed him
And the city did him proud,
Giving him a special place
Of honour in the crowd.

In fact, they hired a gilded boat,
Crested fore and aft,
And wrapped him in a purple rug
(In case of draught).

For even English summers -
You cannot disagree -
Are often so much colder
Than the bottom of the sea.

And there he saw at closest range,
The Undergraduates,
Racing one by one in boats,
     .....In eights.

For all of you must surely know
That Oxford is the place
Where the river is so narrow
That it's hard to have a race.

They do not start dead level,
But single file instead,
And do their very damnedest
To bump the boat ahead.

And in the olden days they used
To bump with such a whack
That often was the cox in front
Speared right in the back.

So just to make for safety
It is customary now
To have a ball or apple
Foremost in the prow!

This is equally effective,
And not at all unkind,
When used to prod the cox in front,
        ....Behind.

And when it all was over
And the sun had ceased to shine,
An elderly and portly Don,
Asked Simon out to dine:

And treated him most graciously,
(Though 'dine' was really 'sup')
And wouldn't let him raise a fin
To assist the washing up.

But all good things must justly end,
And Simon felt that he
Ought to wander downstream
And homewards to the sea.

He said goodbye to all around
And said goodbye again,
Though half a hundred Oxford Dons
Pressed him to remain.

"Please take," they said, "the vacant chair
Of Marine Biology,
With a man to mop your mortarboard
And a maid to make your tea."
Simon shed a tear of pride
And curling round his chair replied:
"Life is really much too short,
Too many things of every sort
Are waiting to be done.
Like swimming out to distant lands,
And listening to silver bands;
And searching for one who understands

Why life was all begun;
And finding girls with golden hair -
Not to talk to, just to stare.
So many wondrous things are there,
And curling round this vacant chair
Is certainly not one."

"Therefore, will you please excuse,
And though I naturally refuse,
You mustn't think that I abuse
Your hospitality.
You see, my nature is marine,
And all my ancestors have been
Connected with the sea.
Yes, all my family before
Have never wandered to the shore,
But served the sea, at arms or law
In some capacity."

"Therefore I must say goodbye,
My new-found friends, for I
Must wend my way with tear and sigh
Downwards on the Thames."
And with these solemn words he went,
With noble send-off he was sent,
With waving hands his barge was spent,
And even willows waved and bent
Their branches from the stems.

Never such a sight was seen.
It never was or will have been
Excelled (except upon the screen).
And every town through which he passed
Received him with a siren blast,
And worked the locks to help him past,
And gave him cups of tea.
To meet him mayors were very proud,
They cheered from bridges long and loud,
Police were called to check the crowd
Which gathered round to see.

Past Abingdon and Wallingford,
Goring, Cleeve and Bourne,
Henley, Hurley, Hambledon,
Late at night and early dawn.
Cookham, Windsor, Romney,
(Where the people paid to look),
Bell Weir, Chertsey, Shepperton,
(Not forgetting Penton Hook).
And the last that I could see of him,
He was swimming past Southend.

And that, my darling children,
            Is the end!

GUM KWOT

A dumb gum kwot
                is not a lot
                of good at a party
        not very hale and not very hearty
                                and gum kwot may,
                                        have nothing to say.

TORTOISE and TURTLE

The tortoise is much less fert'le
than the turtle
This annoys the former
and in climates that are warmer
just eggs the turtle on.

TERRAPIN

                                A terrapin
                        if born too thin
                cannot be saved
                by a safety-pin
        If it flushes
        down the drain
it never will be seen again.

VII

CHIEFLY SUCHLIKE

LULLABY FOR RACHEL

Lullaby my darling
Lullaby my love
Lullaby my angel
Sleep my turtle dove
The arms of night will rock you
The moon will kiss your cheek
So lullaby my darling
Close your eyes and sleep.

1962

NEW YEAR'S GREETINGS

The longitude of platitude
of old and new year greeting
have all been overworked until
they hardly bear repeating.

For maxims mean and mighty
and resolutions by the score
and pithy little sayings
have all been said before.

So glibly said, so soon forgot,
the sad and sorry fact is -
for how much better it would be
to put them into practice.

TORREODOR SONG NEW VERSION

Raise your glasses and your words of praise
To those who risk their lives
Throughout their working days
   Lead on the picador
   Lead on the matador
Then the very bravest of them all
   Will come to the fore.

Who is he who stands out there alone
His life is in his hands
His courage all his own
   He is the Toreador
   He is the Toreador
Yes, the very bravest of them all
   Has come to the fore.

Toreador don't spit upon the floor
Toreador, Toreador
I have told you
Many, many times before
Do not spit on the floor
If you continue so to spit
I'll rub your rotten face in it
So do not spit on the floor!

Apologies to Bizet and others

SALOME
(A SONG)

She's the sigh in Sinai
The apple of Jehovah's eye
She's the girl that makes them cry
Salome Salome Salome

Of creatures in the universe
She's no better, she's no worse
The elders either bless or curse
Salome Salome Salome

If she plays she always wins
Embracing all the seven sins
Where the seventh ends so she begins
Salome Salome Salome

The balm of Gilead's honey and milk,
Rough as a diamond, smooth as silk
Satin skinned and almond eyed
She's the girl who humbled pride
She's no one to be denied
Oh oh oh Salome

A TRIOLET

A   Where have the old time rhymers gone?
B   Singers of the ancient song?
a   is their time past? is their work done?
A   Where have the old time rhymers gone?
a   Was it just they and they alone
b   whose words once carried us along?
A   Where have the old-time rhymers gone?
B   Singers of the ancient song?

December 1990

The saying goes:
'true beauty lies
in the eye
of the beholder',
and this
especially applies
when the woman's
getting older.

Careless woman
with a pram
don't you know
the rules, bedam!
I have much better
things to do
than piling up
my car
on you
although
such sanguine
contemplation
presents a
terrible temptation!

THE WIDOW

Saved by devotion, now she prays
Most of the time on rainy days.
But when its sunny, she asks God's pardon
And busies herself about the garden.

BELIEFS

Perhaps I'm perverse and rather odd
　　　　But I find it hard to believe in God.
There's room for doubt, I will agree
　　　　And I hope that God believes in me.

HYMN

Who is the stranger standing beside me
Whose is the voice that muffles my pain
Whose is the hand that has led me to safety
Over and over and over again.

No longer a stranger is standing beside me
Always a voice that will muffle my pain
And always a hand that will lead me to safety
Over and over and over again.

A PROMISING START

"I'm proud of you, young Wilson
  And the promising start you've made
You have won with flying colours
  And have certainly made the grade.

You started as a factory hand
  And before a month was out
You knew the men and were showing them
  What it was all about.

You went through your apprenticeship
  In a tenth of the time it takes
Then took over our production
  And seldom made mistakes.

With all of these endeavours
  On behalf of the company
A just reward was a seat on the board
  Was plain for all to see.

As junior Director
  Many would agree
Unless I was wrong, it wouldn't be long
  Before you'd be following me.

So now as Chief Executive
  The firm is in your hands,
I'm sure you'll fight with all your might
  To see that it expands."

The young man smiled as he left the room,
He was little more than a lad,
And he paused before he closed the door,
Looked back and said, "Thanks Dad."

If a poet you would be
Indulge in some profanity;
If recognition be your aim
A hopeless passion you should claim;
If publication you desire
Sing lust and passion and hell-fire,
And if, by any chance of fate
You happened once to fornicate
Then write and tell the world about it,
Write it, rhyme it, sing and shout it
For the public love to see
A poet of pornography.
But if, my lad, your only wish
Is to immortalise the fish,
Or deftly flaunt in spoken word
The wild gyrations of a bird;
Or with an agile brush to trace
The passions on the human face,
To take the sorrows that you see
And blend them into poetry
You might as well give up my friend
For me and you it is the end

INDEX OF FIRST LINES

Animals, animals we must unite 54
A dumb gum-kwot is not a lot 66
A terrapin if born too thin 66
A small brow-beaten man he was 33
As roses weep that have no eye to favour 13
Autumn at Kew in a breath-held stillness 2
A zoom bazoo bazoo 36

Back from church the people come 27
Bring my gun and cartridges 58

Can you hear the singing bird 23
Careless woman with a pram 70

Duck-billed platypus dancing on a
   dandelion 53

Fall into my arms beloved 6
Farewell delightful evening 4

Go placidly, go placidly 74

Harsh, like a ranting bark vibrating 28
Have you ever heard the tale 59
Have you lost love, O intellectual one 15
Higher and higher in the city 37
How should I love you 9

I asked the way to heaven 38
I cannot hear the cuckoo calling 30
I did not mean to love you 8
I like the way you stand, you silken slut 28
I sat, where we sat, those years ago 22
I saw a woman with a lovely face 33
I smile on you, for you are lovely 10
I'm proud of you young Wilson 71
If a poet you should be 72
If I should die in Bedford 26
If only my love had been fine and fair 18
If your breasts were towers of ivory 11
I've come ten thousand miles to hear those
   bells 24

Jill jilted me, I'm sad to say 19

Kiss me while the going's good 19

Lie here unnamed, unknown, in shallow
   rest 31
Lullaby my darling 67

Mavis, gentle Mavis 21
"Mind the doors," he said distinctly 39
Miss Arzopardi, though your face 40
Morning in the City 37
My little sister Marion 57
My love is like a red, red rose 16
My verse is not profound, enigmatical vi

Not with a sigh you gave yourself to me 13

Of small and slender stature though my
   mistress be 8

Pathetic little sparrow, must you die 58
Perhaps I'm perverse and rather odd 70

Raise your glasses and your words of
   praise 68
Rejoice there'll be an end to dying 50

Saved by devotion, now she prays 70
She, in his arms, lay 7
She's the sigh in Sinai 69
She said it would be best for her to go 17
She turned and kissed me where I stood 11
Six days a week, the whole year through 34
Softly the branches ply 29
So great a man 42
So this is the new world order 49
Stay with me Bridget, here may we 4

Take it while the sap is rising 1
The Clapham boys are spunky 29
The chimney stacks of Sandy 30
The girls of Potten, Sandy, Beds 29
The gods she followed were death
   foreboding 17

The longitude of platitude 67
The saying goes "true beauty lies. . ." 70
This counterpane of sorrows 32
The teeming streets of Oxford 45
The tortoise is much less firt'le that the
   turtle 66
There is a cruel emptiness 14
There is a time and place in life 18
There is no majesty for man 41
To each and all by love or sorrow torn 3
To Putnoe Woods in springtime 35

We have a secret no-one shares 21
What use of pride 32
When all is said and all is done 46
When the oak be lightning riven 12
Where Indian princes walked and passed
   their day 52
Where have the old time rhymers gone? 69
Why should I try when others fail? 5
Who is that stranger standing beside me 70
Who will walk in the meadow 44

You turned and kissed me 13
Young woman in a yellow dress 43

GO PLACIDLY

Go placidly, go placidly
Amid life's noise and haste
Silence, a rare commodity,
Is not a thing to waste.

Without surrender or abuse
Endeavour if you can
To keep good terms in daily use
With each and every man.

Speak your truth, but quietly,
Let others speak to you
Even the dull and ignorant
They have their story too.